W9-CYZ-151

This is a Dorling Kindersley Book
published by Random House, Inc.

Senior Editor Jane Yorke
Editor Charlotte Davies
Art Editor Toni Rann
Designer Heather Blackham
Photography Stephen Oliver
Additional Photography Tim Ridley, Stephen Shott
Series Consultant Neil Morris
Hand Model Lewis Blitz

First American edition, 1991

Published in the United States by Random House, Inc., New York.
This edition first published in Great Britain by
Dorling Kindersley Publishers Limited in 1991.

Library of Congress Cataloging-in-Publication Data
My first look at counting.
p. cm.

Summary: Photographs of fruits, toys, and other objects
introduce the concept of counting.
ISBN 0-679-81163-X
1. Counting – Juvenile literature. 2. Counting. I. Random House (Firm)
II. Title: Counting.
QA113. M93 1991
513.5'5 – dc20
[E]
90-8577 CIP AC

Manufactured in Italy 1 2 3 4 5 6 7 8 9 10

Reproduced by Bright Arts, Hong Kong
Printed and bound in Italy by L.E.G.O.

· MY · FIRST · LOOK · AT ·

Counting

Random House New York

Counting up

Can you count from one to ten?

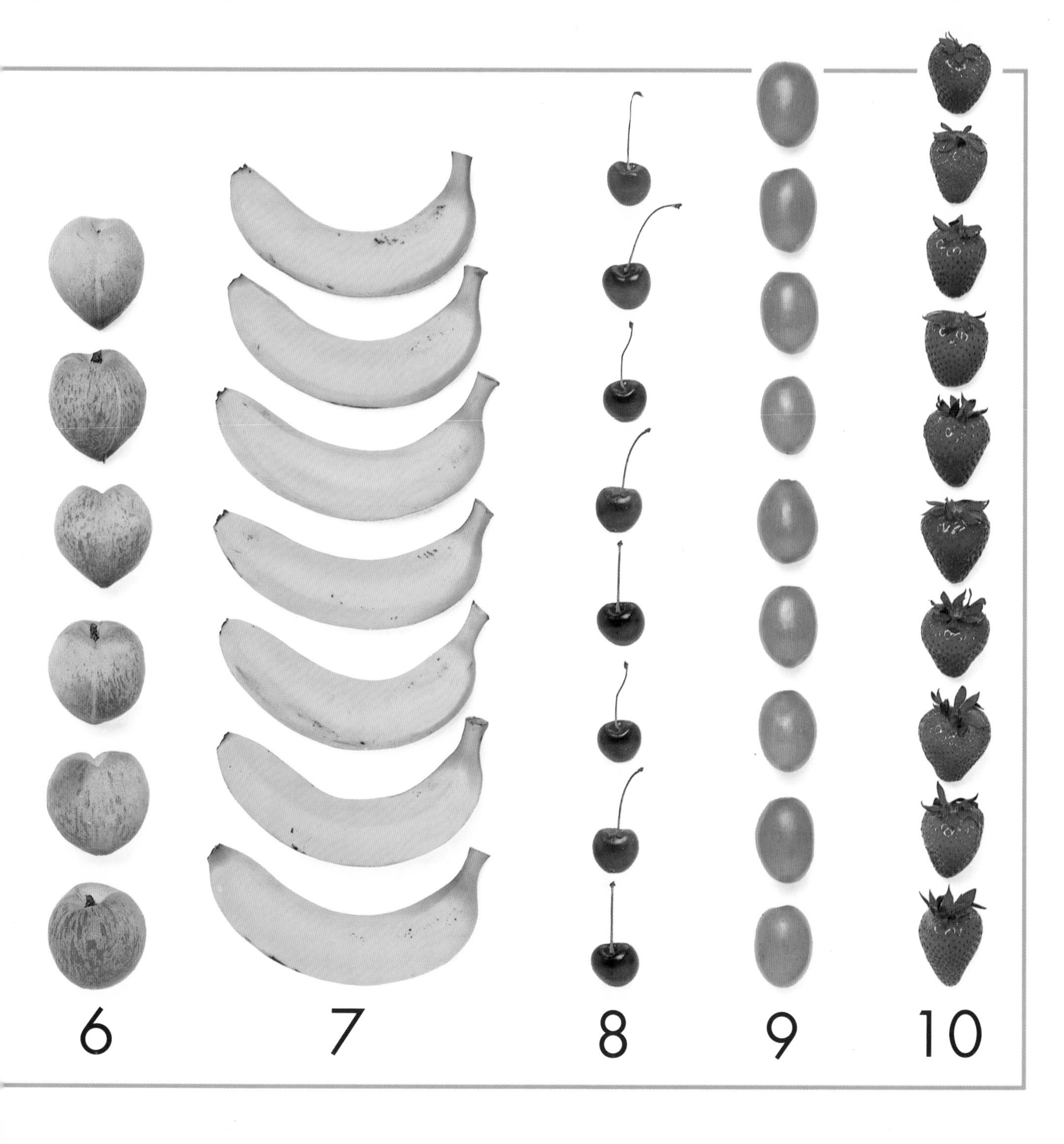
6
7
8
9
10

How many?

How many flowers
can you count?

How many mugs are there?

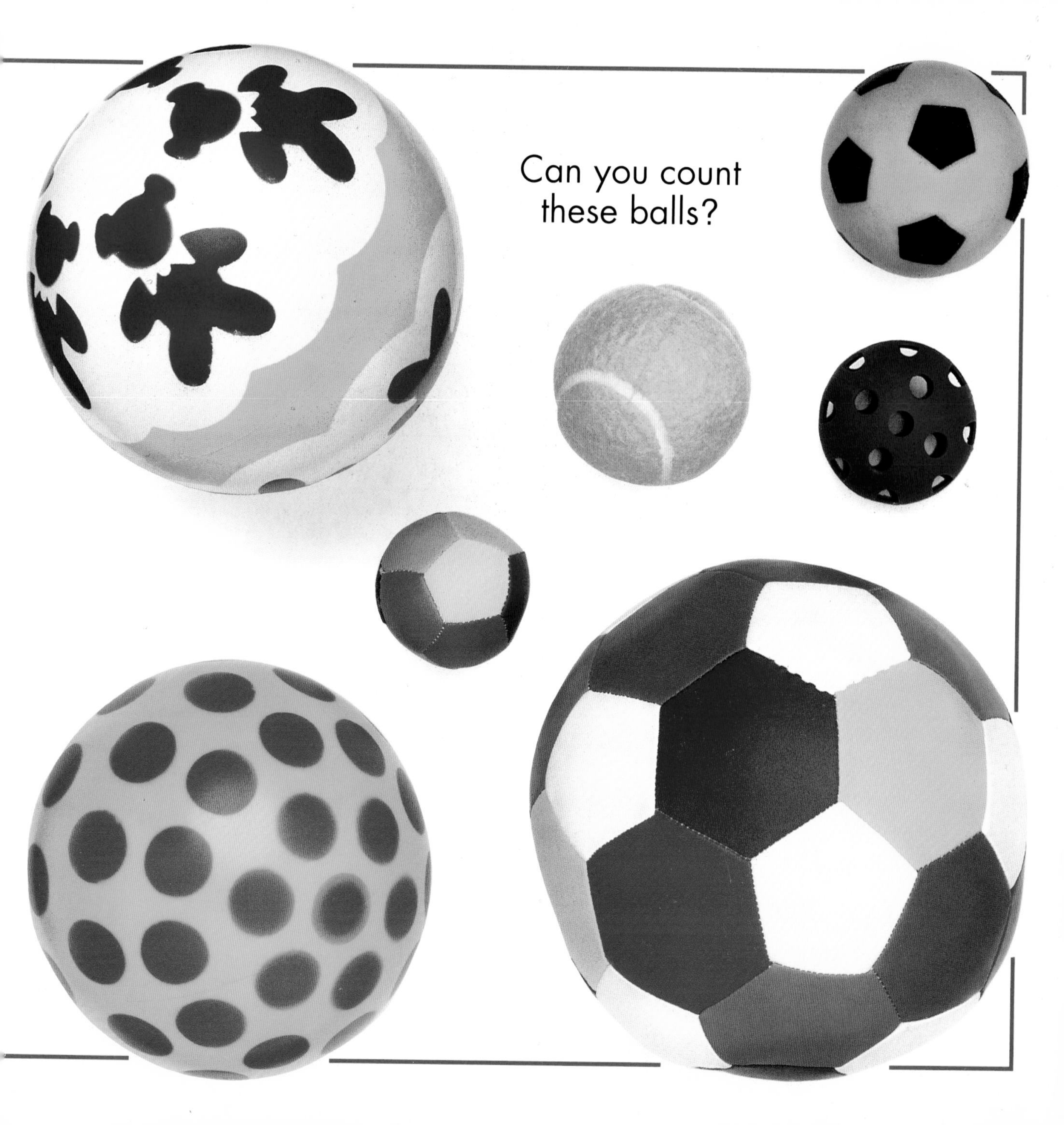
Can you count
these balls?

Counting cars

How many red cars are there?

How many blue cars?

How many cars are there altogether?

Counting toys

Can you count the teddy bears?

Can you count the airplanes?

Can you count
all the toys together?

Counting shapes

How many round things
can you count?

blocks

picture

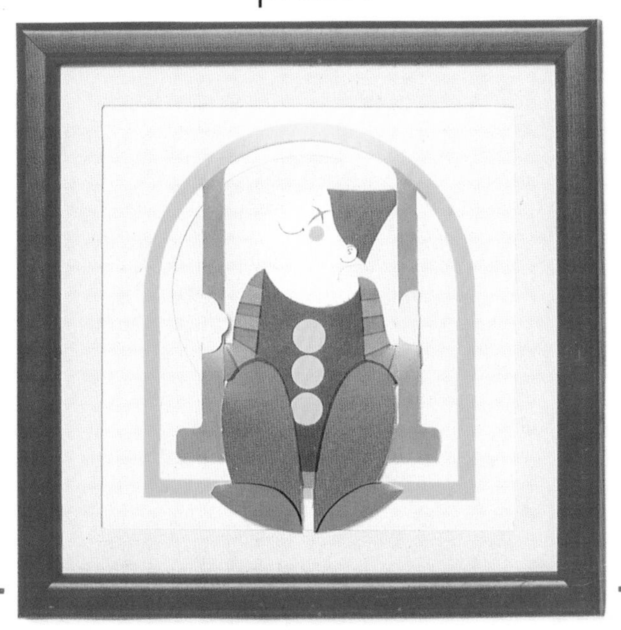

shopping bag

doorknob

ball of yarn

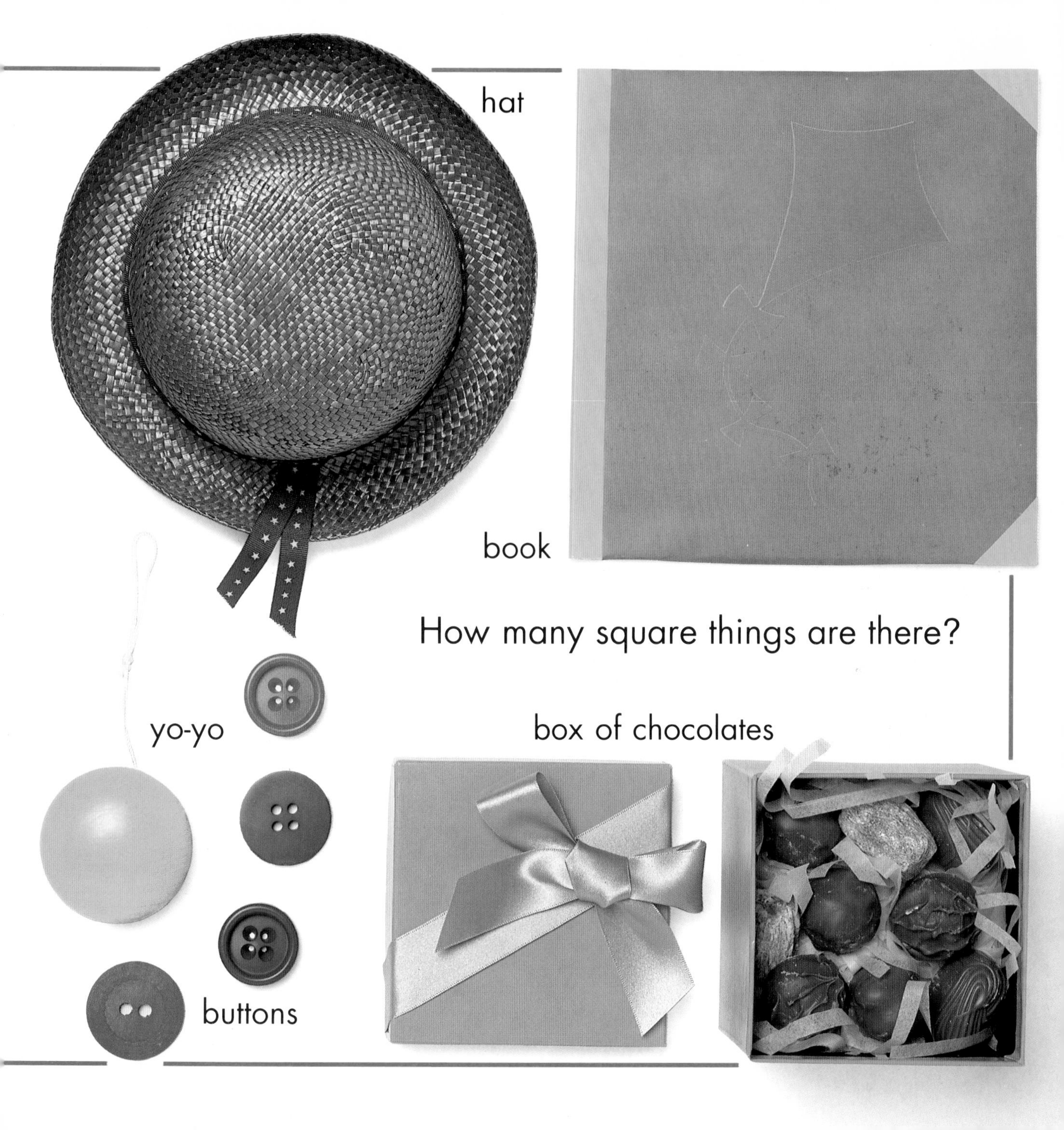
hat
book
How many square things are there?
yo-yo
box of chocolates
buttons

Adding apples

How many apples can you count?

How many are there now?

Cutting the cake

How many slices of cake are there?

How many slices have been eaten?
How many slices are left?

At the seaside

How many shells are there?